Supporting Student Personal Learning Networks

by Lisa Nielsen
and her
Personal Learning Network

an imprint of Eifrig Publishing
Lemont   Berlin

Supporting Student Personal Learning Networks

by Lisa Nielsen
and her
Personal Learning Network

© 2021 by Lisa Nielsen
Printed in the United States of America

All rights reserved. This publication is protected by Copyright, and permission should be obtained from the publisher prior to any prohibited reproduction, storage in a retrieval system, or transmission in any form or by any means, electronic, mechanical, photocopying, recording, or likewise.

Published by Eifrig Publishing,
PO Box 66, Lemont, PA 16851.
Knobelsdorffstr. 44, 14059 Berlin, Germany

For information regarding permission, write to:
Rights and Permissions Department,
Berry Street Books, an imprint of Eifrig Publishing,
PO Box 66, Lemont, PA 16851, USA.
permissions@eifrigpublishing.com, 888-340-6543.

Library of Congress Cataloging-in-Publication Data

Nielsen, Lisa,

  Supporting Student Personal Learning Networks / by Lisa Nielsen.
     p.   cm.

Paperback ISBN: 978-1-63233-085-7
Ebook ISBN: 978-1-63233-086-4

  1. Education 2. Student Personal Learning
  I. Nielsen, Lisa, II. Title.

25 24 23 22 2021
5 4 3 2 1

Printed on acid-free paper. ∞

The Innovative Educator Series

Fix the School, Not the Child: 20 Ideas for Parents Who Want to Advocate for the Rights of their Child in School
ISBN 978-1-936172-88-7 ($7.99)

Building a Strong Home-School Connection with Cell Phones (with Willyn Webb)
ISBN 978-1-63233-005-5 ($7.99)

How to Opt Out (Not Drop Out) of School: A Guide for Teens for Self-Directed Education
ISBN 978-1-63233-048-2 ($7.99)

Supporting Student Personal Learning Networks
ISBN 978-1-63233-085-7 ($7.99)

The Uncomfortable History of American Schooling: 1500s -Today
ISBN 978-1-63233-091-8 ($7.99)

The Social Classroom: Engaging Learners with Cell Phones & Social Media
ISBN 978-1-63233-089-5 ($7.99)

The Working Home Educator's Guide to Success: Stories and Advice for Working Families That Want to Home Educate
ISBN 978-1-63233-087-1 ($7.99)

Educators are connecting on Twitter, Facebook, Instagram, blogs, Google Hangouts and more, as they develop personal learning networks as a tool for professional growth. Personal Learning Networks (PLNs) are those connections individual learners make to suit their specific perceived learning needs. With the internet at our disposal, location is no longer a barrier to building solid and productive relationships; interest, knowledge and enthusiasm are all that's needed.

PLNs have become popular with educators because they are a fantastic way to receive anytime/anywhere professional development and support in their area of interest.

At school, some educators may have only a few people who share their specialty and little time to connect; librarians, speech teachers, technology teachers, etc., are often the only such practitioner in a building. PLNs provide them not only with information and insight, but access to other practitioners, leaders and experts. Mutual excitement and deep interest on similar subjects brings together communities, resources and information otherwise inaccessible from within the walls of an unconnected school, workplace, or community.

Educators know that in today's world, value is found in more than just what you know; *who you know* and *how to make the most* of those connections and information is even more important. This holds true for youth as well. If we want young people to achieve success in the world today, we must step up and support students as they build their own 21st century rolodex, the PLN. While it is not unusual to find educators who have an extensive network consisting of bloggers they read and/or comment on, those they chat with on Twitter, and those they see and chat with on Google Hangouts, most educators have not helped their students develop PLNs of their own.

What is ubiquitous as a tool for entertainment and personal fulfillment has not yet been considered by the mainstream as a source of professional innovation.

That's not to say students aren't doing this. They are. But it is often without the potentially useful guidance and support of caring and trusted adults. As I began to write this chapter, I found no shortage of students eager to share how they built and developed their PLNs. I had a harder time finding teachers who support students in this effort. The teachers you will hear from, below, are doing pioneering work and will provide insights and inspiration for others. Most difficult to locate were the parents who support their children's PLN development. I reached out to parents via Twitter, Facebook, and email. I found very few. As you'll find below, many of those I did find have utilized PLNs as one in a series of non-traditional learning choices for their children, foremost among them *unschooling*, a form of homeschooling where the talents, passions and strengths of the learner take a front seat to instruction. These families say that the PLNs of their children are usually invisible; they are just a natural way their children connect with others. Several even refer to their PLN development as "accidental."

However, while the children of some parents may have stumbled onto it, it is beneficial for all parents to be deliberately supportive of their child's learning network. This requires exposure to the concept as well as ideas they can use to support their children. Teachers can be the crucial facilitators of this exposure.

Contributors

The educators and parents you will hear from in this chapter explain how they support the young people in their lives with PLN development. You will also hear from some amazing teens. They share with us the importance of personal learning networks not only to their academic and career success, but also to their success in impacting the world in meaningful ways. Below are the names of the students, teachers, and parents who will share with you their strategies, methods, and ideas that lead to the successful development of a personal learning network.

Students
Courtney Gressman @CGressmanTHS
Connor Wood
Alex Laubscher http://instagram.com/alex_laubscher
Nikhil Goyal @nikhilgoya_l
Zak Malamed @zakmal
Jabreel Chisley @enragedstudent
Armond McFadden | @Originality_Flx

Educators
Ann S. Michaelsen @annmic
Adam Taylor @2footgiraffe

Kendra Burnett Tiemann
Linda Yollis @lindayollis
Courtney Woods @CourtneyM_Woods
Angela Maiers @AngelaMaiers

Parents
Amy Milstein @greenmangoes
Lainie Liberti @ilainie
Kelly Raudenbush @myoverthinking
Lisa Nalbone @lisanalbone
Dana Britt | @Dana_Britt
Jennifer Laubscher @JenLaubscher
Dayna Martin @YourTwitterHandle

Students

On the following pages you will hear from some amazing teens, each of whom has developed a personal learning network to pursue their passion. You'll hear from students like Courtney Gressman, who wants to open the eyes and minds of educators as to how students feel about school. Cartoonist Alex Laubscher shares the importance of his PLN in helping to make his dream of having his work become a household name come true. Learn from teen author Nikhil Goyal who blasts schools for their lack of support: "There wasn't a single opportunity to meet people outside the school bubble. It's absurd how restrictive schools are."

As you read the insights from these incredible young people pay special attention to the advice they have for educators and parents in supporting their efforts.

Contributor	
Courtney Gressman @CGressmanTHIS	Tarrant High School C/O 2015. Varsity Cheerleader, Youth Leader Future Psychologist/Business Manager. Tarrant, Al.
Questions	
Why did you build a PLN?	I built a personal learning network because I felt that there has been an obvious problem in schools that needed to be taken care of, and that to find a solution to this problem more people needed to get together and see how students feel about this.
How did you build your PLN i.e. What platforms did you use and how?	I built my PLN by creating a video on YouTube called "Learning is Natural. The Way We Learn Should Be Optional" http://youtu.be/sMsGu2sf7Yw. Just publishing on YouTube isn't enough though. You have to find your audience. I did that by going to Twitter and using hashtags like #EducationReform and #Education to find educators who might be interested. I tweeted my video to them, engaged in conversations, and started following them. One such educator partnered with me to share my work on her blog, The Innovative Educator (InnovativeEducator.com).
How has your PLN helped you / what you care about grow?	My PLN has given me more insight into how many educators are interested in what students think about how we are learning. I've also gained more knowledge about how to create a PLN.

Student Personal Learning Networks

Share a couple of the most powerful examples of how your PLN has been of value.	The most powerful examples of how my PLN has been of value are when I see educators outside of my district, and even my state, positively comment on the video I created saying that they agree and wish more students would speak their mind on this. It is also meaningful when the students in my school say that they want this to be fixed as well. It shows that this not only a problem locally, but nationally, and that I'm not the only one who wants to take a stand against it.
Did (or would you) meet members of your PLN face-to-face? If so, how was that / why might you want to? How did you know it was safe to do so?	I have spoken to a few educators and education reformers involved in my PLN. It was so much easier to speak freely with them and understand their ideas and goals on what they are involved in. It was a lot better than being on a 140 character limit. We knew these hangouts were safe because they were set up by our teacher, who had known them for a while before we met them.
What is your advice for adults stuck in the mindset that you should never meet someone face-to-face that you've only met online?	I would tell them that though there are dangers, there are also ways to prevent bad things from happening. Although by definition student personal learning networks are student-made, ideally there is a teacher involved as well. This would mean that the student is supported by a teacher and would get his/her help before planning to meet with online connections.
Was your school involved in the development of your PLN? If so, how? If not, what could your school have done to support you?	My school was involved in the development of my PLN. This began as just a project for my social studies class (#SandersTHS) but then grew into something I truly cared about. My teacher (@MsSandersTHS on Twitter) guided me with the tools to plan and create the beginning of my PLN.

Have your parents been involved in the development of your PLN? If so, how? If not would you want their support and how might you want them to support you?	My mother has supported my PLN by sharing my video and twitter to some of her close friends on Facebook as well as showing a lot of people in person who later responded online. She has also given me her personal support and encouragement. She let me know that I was doing a wonderful job when I thought that the issue behind my PSA wasn't going to be that relevant and reminded me that I could do anything I wanted as long as I set my mind to it while I was building my PLN. This encouraged me to keep going and responding to as many people as possible.
What else do you feel is important in the area of student personal learning networks?	When students create PLN, they are actively preparing themselves for the future no matter what career they go into. It allows them to learn how to utilize their tools, speak their mind on something they really care about, and communicate effectively with others about it. This is something people use in all sorts of different careers, whether it be education, business, etc. I believe that is the most important thing of all.

Contributor	
Connor Wood Blogger at: tri-nab-tu-we.blogspot.com/.	Student and education activist. Founder of West High Student Union, organizing an anthology of student reactions to their education.
Questions	
Why did you build a PLN?	I didn't really mean to. I just started contacting people with questions after realizing something had to be done about our education system. I just hoped to gain some better idea of what was going on. Along the way, some people like James Bach and Jerry Mintz were really helpful. I asked them some more questions, started taking their advice, found some more people, and then I found myself with a group of people who could help me. I wasn't working to reform by myself anymore.

How did you build your PLN i.e. What platforms did you use and how?	Aside from my blog, Google+ is the only social network I use, and I only use that for important posts on my blog. I guess I am kind of old school in that when I started going around looking for people to interview, I used only email. Since a lot of people put their email online, it was simple to find people to address my questions. From there I got the idea to do a series of interviews for my blog. Eventually, I had ten, including James Bach, Diane Ravitch, Conrad Wolfram and Lisa Nielsen. Through these interviews, a lot of people offered their advice and suggestions. Then I have those friends who are just as committed as I am, but would rather work behind the scenes. They can give me instant feedback. So school is a good place to look for help.
How has your PLN helped you / what you care about grow?	With a lot of hard work and some patience, people are starting to listen to me. I even had a meeting with the head principal of my school about some policy changes and questions I addressed in the open letter I published on my blog about policy changes. They had policy, but now because of my blog and my learning network, I had the connections and voice that led to publicity. The more support my actions gain, the more people will follow, seeing in my concerns ways of addressing their own problems. Once students learn to speak for themselves, education will change for the better.

Student Personal Learning Networks

Share a couple of the most powerful examples of how your PLN has been of value.	One way my PLN has been of value is with providing me with support to create my education blog Trismegistus Nab-tu-we. I contacted author Henry Olsen and entrepreneur William Peregoy and asked them for advice. They were both helpful in giving me the tools and ideas I needed to start my blog and autodidactism. There were also two student groups I have turned to Students for Education Reform and The Providence Student Union. Both provided valuable advice for maintaining my blog successfully.
Did (or would you) meet members of your PLN face-to-face? If so, how was that / why might you want to? How did you know it was safe to do so?	One of the great things about the internet is that like the blogosphere, it has the power to connect people worldwide. This allows us to meet the minds of those we otherwise would likely never have had the chance to connect with in the physical world. When major people in my network live thousands of miles away, face-to-face meetings are a little difficult. While I did do a phone interview with a representative from the Students for Education Reform, I have never had the opportunity to meet anyone face-to-face who I originally met online. That is not to say that I don't want to. In fact, at some point I plan to.

What is your advice for adults stuck in the mindset that you should never meet someone face-to-face that you've only met online?	I have also been armed with the knowledge to interact with those I've only met online safely. Growing up in the internet era, I spent a considerable portion of my childhood being told to be careful online. One should not give away certain information and never meet someone in person who one has only met online. Of course, that is somewhat impractical, since if one has never known the stranger personally, by that rule, one never can. It also assumes that the only way to know someone is if you are physically in the same space. PLNs thrive when you get to know someone's ideas through communicating online. However, one should show some discretion. If he or she refuses to give you a real name, insist on meeting in an alley, and tells one to be sure to come alone, it might be a good idea not to go. However, I think that if you connected with that person through a reputable site, or even through another contact, you should be fine. Common sense is still a valuable thing.

Was your school involved in the development of your PLN? If so, how? If not, what could your school have done to support you?	I originally started the blog as a project for my high school English class. Unlike my classmates, who quit after the three posts required by my teacher, I kept going a while, trying to turn it into another type of blog. I talked about books, languages, liberal arts, programming, and internet culture. Then I got into politics, and I still do, occasionally. I covered a whole mess of things. But it was not regular. I realized from my page-views that without consistency and focus my blog did not seem to be worth anybody's time. My blog had progressed from a class project, to random musings, and now it had a focus. It has become a blog about changing school in general. I am currently in the process of doing a series of interviews with various people on education reform.
Have your parents been involved in the development of your PLN? If so, how? If not would you want their support and how might you want them to support you?	My parents haven't really been involved at all. They let me set up my blog, start the West High Student Union, and allow me to try to start a writing career. After that, they just let me go. That is nice. This way I can fail. I have to be my own safety net. I'll learn from my own mistakes, rather than from their mistakes. I need to be independent to learn from this, and they are giving me that chance by being non-interventionist in this.

What else do you feel is important in the area of student personal learning networks?	Do not limit your network to one field. A number of people in my PLN have nothing to do with education reform. But they have valuable ideas, and are interesting people to boot. If you sense a kindred spirit, introduce yourself. It is not the "learning" part that is important as much as it is the "personal." One can have a network of the top people in one's own field, but if one cannot talk to those people about anything else, what is the point?

Student Personal Learning Networks

Contributor	
Alex Laubscher instagram.com/alex laubscher	Create more. Zine culture. Comics life. Coffee. RIP Kurt High School Freshman Syracuse, NY
Questions	
Why did you build a PLN?	My dream is to be a cartoonist. I want my work and characters to be moderately household names in the comic culture and zine community. Creating my PLN has helped me with this dream. I'm proud to say that there are many zinesters and artists that know and follow my work pretty consistently.
How did you build your PLN i.e. What platforms did you use and how?	There were many ways that I created my PLN. The most useful one has been my Instagram page, where I post photos and videos of a multitude of things. I post my creative process, finished product, and mini comics and zines I've received from fellow artists via trade. Another platform I have used is a site called wemakezines.ning.com, which is basically a Facebook for zinesters. I also explore other creator websites, blogs, and tumblrs, where I can usually ask questions directly through the site, or find an email address. I also have many fans and readers who attend my high school.

How has your PLN helped you / what you care about grow?	My PLN is the reason I have a fan-base. I've developed relationships with many people through trades and social media. My PLN has exposed me to many different forms and styles of art and writing. It's given me inspiration. I always look forward to hearing peoples' opinions and receiving new reading material
Share a couple of the most powerful examples of how your PLN has been of value.	I think that it's really cool to just be part of a culture. My PLN has been a doorway to a lifestyle filled with amazing writers, artists and other creators that would have been invisible to me without it. I'm building my zine library, and when I browse through my books the word that flashes through my mind as I flip through the papers is culture. It's amazing. People are being exposed to my work all over the world: places all around America, like California, and Texas, and Ohio etc... or other places overseas like the UK, Australia, Puerto Rico, Singapore, China... it's really just amazing.

Student Personal Learning Networks

Did (or would you) meet members of your PLN face-to-face? If so, how was that / why might you want to? How did you know it was safe to do so?	I've never met members of my PLN other than my family and the readers that attend my school or live locally, but if I had a chance to meet some of the acquaintances from online I definitely would. It would nice for many reasons. Currently, I am working on a collaboration story with a fellow cartoonist that would be much easier to work on if we were in the same room. I think that through platforms like Instagram, Facebook and Tumblr, after a long while its kind of apparent the kind of people they are. I have been emailing many of these people for a long time. Plus, I like to think that I have slightly good judgment so with all these factors I think it would be safe if one of these opportunities of meeting occurred.
What is your advice for adults stuck in the mindset that you should never meet someone face-to-face that you've only met online?	My advice is that you should use your head and common sense. There are ways to know if its right to meet someone and there are safe ways to do it. For example, my mother and I met a couple from Italy online during a Home Exchange and now we are great friends. They visit in the summer and stay in our house. We visit them and stay in Rome. Rob thinks of me of his little brother and I think of him the same way. It would be horrible if I didn't have these people in my life, They are people who are now my family, because my mom was not stuck in the mindset that you should never meet anyone from online.

Was your school involved in the development of your PLN? If so, how? If not, what could your school have done to support you?	Yes, sort of a few. Yeah. But not all teachers. I've created zines solely for assignments in a few classes as an alternate assignment. I also have art teachers that have been incredibly supportive. In fact, they have actually given me more than half of the art supplies I own. For example, the Assistant Principal has purchased every issue of my STRIP(er) that I have created and reached out to a friend in the comic book business to ask if he had any advice to pass along to me. He's been really supportive, especially since it's against school policy to sell anything on school grounds and they've been behind it a hundred percent. My guidance counselor helps me get my books copied and stapled. It's amazing.
Have your parents been involved in the development of your PLN? If so, how? If not would you want their support and how might you want them to support you?	Not really. My mom did encourage me to use Instagram but I mainly developed my learning network on my own.

Student Personal Learning Networks

Contributor	
Nikhil Goyal @nikhilgoya_1	18-Year-Old Author and Activist. New York · nikhilgoyal.me
Questions	
How and why did you build a PLN? What platforms did you use and how?	I didn't build my PLN in a conscious manner. In other words, I didn't realize that I was creating a PLN. For example, on Twitter, I just began following people who share provocative links and views and those who have similar interests to mine. I've tried to limit the number of people I followed so that I can interact with a smaller group of people more regularly.
How has your PLN helped you / what you care about grow? Provide some examples of how this has been of value.	My PLN has helped me tremendously. Some portions of the research of my [books](#) have come from reading links to articles or books posted by people in my learning network. Last year, when I was looking for a web designer, I posted on Twitter my request and included my email address and got more than ten responses within hours. I also get some great reading recommendations from my PLN. I often like to tweet as I read a book and often times, someone sends a link to a similar book on the topic.

Did (or would you) meet members of your PLN face-to-face? If so, how was that / why might you want to? How did you know it was safe to do so?	It's a truly wonderful experience meeting people that you engage with online in person. It adds another layer to your relationship. This often happens at conferences or events or simply deciding to meet for coffee or a meal. This was safe, because you're meeting this person in a setting with lots of other people. It's also important that the person has a public profile to verify information. This is not similar to messaging strangers on instant messaging services, like AIM. In this case, you would know where the person lives, what their job is, and most importantly, their mutual friends.
What is your advice for adults stuck in the mindset that you should never meet someone face-to-face that you've only met online?	I would suggest trying to meet people in your PLN in a public place: a coffee shop, restaurant, bookstore, etc.
Was your school involved in the development of your PLN? If so, how? If not, what could your school have done to support you?	My school did nothing to help grow my PLN. Social media was blocked in school. There wasn't a single opportunity to meet people outside of the school bubble. It's absurd how restrictive schools are.
Have your parents been involved in the development of your PLN? If so, how? If not, would you want their support & how could they best support you?	My parents aren't involved in the development of my PLN. They aren't very active on social media.

Student Personal Learning Networks

Contributor	
Zak Malamed @ zakmal	Founder & E.D. of @Stu_Voice. On Mondays at 8:30pm EDT, I use #StuVoice a lot. @UofMaryland '16. Zak@StuVoice.org NYC & Washington D.C. · StuVoice.org
Questions	
Why did you build a PLN?	I started a PLN because I realized the lack of voice students had in designing their educational experience and I wanted to discover people who shared my belief in the critical value student voices have in creating a high quality educational experience.
How did you build your PLN i.e. What platforms did you use and how?	I used Twitter by following hashtags in the education community and thereafter, interacting with individuals using those hashtags. I also created the #StuVoice hashtag to formulate a community for my own PLN. Beyond Twitter, there are many Facebook groups like Student Voice and The Innovative Educator that pool together people interested in connecting and sharing ideas.
How has your PLN helped you / what you care about grow?	My PLN indirectly grew into a not-for-profit organization, Student Voice. This came from substantial investment in the PLN from people and other organizations
Share a couple of the most powerful examples of how your PLN has been of value.	We have continued to host weekly #StuVoice chats on Twitter on Monday nights at 8:30pm EST. We are making StuVoice.org the hub for those who are or can invest in student voices, and have also organized Student Voice Live!, an international conference that reached upwards of 5 million and had satellite events on 22 countries across six continents.

Did (or would you) meet members of your PLN face-to-face. If so, how was that / why might you want to? How did you know it was safe to do so?	Yes, that's exactly why Student Voice Live! took place. Digital relationships are valuable, but we form stronger connections and learn so much more from each other when we have the opportunity to meet in person. I felt safe doing so because of the authenticity that each person's story carried throughout my PLN.
What is your advice for adults stuck in the mindset that you should never meet someone face-to-face that you've only met online?	Meeting people online is just the nature of the 21st Century. Simply put, the good that comes out of relationships formed online far outweighs the bad that you hear about in the news. It is the responsibility of our community and more specifically, that of our schools to not only teach students how to be safe online, but also about how to use the Internet to their advantage. This is an essential skill in a 21st Century society and we can only best learn how to teach students and each other through experiencing ourselves the realities of how people are utilizing the Internet.
Was your school involved in the development of your PLN? If so, how? If not, what could your school have done to support you?	No. Schools need to teach students how to use the Internet to their advantage. Most of what was taught in school I had already learned on my own. Schools need to open doors for students to start learning how to leverage online social tools in the most effective manner possible.

Student Personal Learning Networks

H Have your parents been involved in the development of your PLN? If so, how? If not, would you want their support & how could they best support you?	My parents were originally skeptical of how I was leveraging Twitter, but when they saw my PLN in person, they realized how incredible a PLN can be and how far it can take a student like me. Their greatest support was in allowing me to explore and experience the value of a PLN, while many parents still hold their children back from experiencing such things.
What else do you feel is important in the area of student personal learning networks?	The classroom is no longer constricted by its four walls. You can learn just as much from a student in Dubai as you can from a student sitting right next to you.

Contributor	
Jabreel Chisley @ enragedstudent	19 year-old blogger from East Cleveland, OH who's passionate about social justice and educational equality.
Questions	
Why did you build a PLN?	I never had any intention on building a PLN, it just happened.
How did you build your PLN i.e. What platforms did you use and how?	My PLN all traces back to one person actually, David Loitz. He is the first person I recall coming in contact with. It grew when I shared my story on an education blog called the Cooperative Catalyst (http://coopcatalyst.wordpress.com) and it just kept growing the more I shared my ideas and beliefs.
How has your PLN helped you / what you care about grow?	My PLN consists of people who like to know why and how...and because of that I have found myself digging deeper for a more informed understanding of issues I am interested in from multiple perspectives. This is how I found myself interested in the School to Prison Pipeline and Feminist issues within the public school.
Share a couple of the most powerful examples of how your PLN has been of value.	When I first became involved in the conversation around issues such as equality in schools. I was very naive about how open everyone would be. While the majority of the people are open minded, there are a few who are not. My PLN has been a valuable tool in learning how to deal with those who are not open to different opinions and perspectives.

Did (or would you) meet members of your PLN face-to face? If so, how was that / why might you want to? How did you know it was safe to do so?	I've actually met members of my PLN multiple times. It was an awesome experience every time because it allows you to gain a understanding of the people who have an influence on you in a more casual situation. I knew it was safe because everyone in my PLN had a verifiable background and they were all consistent.
What is your advice for adults stuck in the mindset that you should never meet someone face-to-face that you've only met online?	It's something to do with extreme caution and hesitation. I suggest that adults sit down with youth and together figure out if everyone in their PLN is "on the up and up." I don't think it is something that should never happen though...the world is too big to pass up the chance to meet people who share the same interest.
Was your school involved in the development of your PLN? If so, how? If not, what could your school have done to support you?	My school wasn't directly involved in my PLN but they were supportive of it. As long as I could prove I was on to something productive and could find a way to get myself to events they were actually pretty intrigued by it.
Have your parents been involved in the development of your PLN? If so, how? If not would you want their support and how should they support you?	My parent was actually not very supportive of my PLN, mostly because she didn't understand what the conversations we had were centered around. However, her support would have been very useful, as it would have allowed me to become better acquainted with more people.
What else do you feel is important in the area of student personal learning networks?	Confidence and acceptance. These are two things that are important in developing and keeping a PLN. Not everyone will agree with you and you won't agree with everyone but that does not make the views of others any less important.

Contributor	
Armond McFadden | @Originality_Flx	I am a 19-year old college Sophomore in New York City who is passionate about transportation and photography. I enjoy what I do and love to inform others about what I do.
Questions	
Why did you build a PLN?	I chose to build a PLN because I wanted people to know more about what I have to offer and what I'm into. I look at a PLN as a more personal and direct way of people getting to know what I'm about. Also potential employers and events at school such as Job Fairs which other people come from other places to pick out students who stand out and they love to look at PLN's.
How did you build your PLN i.e. What platforms did you use and how?	Right now I am using websites like Flickr to post my digital photography photos as well as YouTube which is where I post my videos and share with others. Also http://about.me/metro.transit.vids is a great website because it shows all my important links in one place for others to see. LinkedIn (http://www.linkedin.com/pub/armond-mcfadden/61/764/a23 is also an important place for me because it is a great way to connect with others who share your professional interests.
How has your PLN helped you / what you care about grow?	My PLN has helped me with my hobby for Mass Transportation because it shows the world what I'm about and it motivates others to do the same as well. Find your knack and make yourself known in the digital world because that's what people look at, especially employers.

Student Personal Learning Networks

Share a couple of the most powerful examples of how your PLN has been of value.	I am able to go back to my middle school where I first started taking steps into the digital world and share with others how my PLN has helped me and inspire them to think about growing their own network. I also had a job interview with the Apple store before I took steps into the workforce and although I didn't have working experience at the time, the interviewer was amazed how connected I was. She appreciated what she saw. I will apply again for Apple very soon since I have more experience now.
Did (or would you) meet members of your PLN face-to-face? If so, how was that / why might you want to? How did you know it was safe to do so?	I haven't met anybody yet in person but I have met Ms. Lisa Nielsen online which inspired me to take my passion and push forward with the support of my PLN.
What is your advice for adults stuck in the mindset that you should never meet someone face-to-face that you've only met online?	My advice is to be bold, be smart, and not afraid for opportunity. You never know what the person has to offer unless you take a chance. It is a great experience to meet new people and exchange ideas because in my opinion two (or more!) heads are better than one.

Was your school involved in the development of your PLN? If so, how? If not, what could your school have done to support you?	My high school wasn't exactly focused on supporting me in building my PLN but they focused on technology in other helpful ways including creating a digital resume. The focus was more on writing and literature. I was in a computer repair program so I focused on that area as well. My middle school was different. They were a perfect school because they supported and encouraged me in developing my PLN. They were focused on helping me find and grow my talents, passions, and interests. They connected me to a variety of online outlets such as blogging. Schools can support students in developing their PLNs by making sure they know how to take ownership of their online identity using platforms like blogging and YouTube. It would be ideal if a school principal was able to model how they use their PLN then stress the importance of it to teachers outlining what steps they can take to incorporate it into their lessons and make learning fun.
Have your parents been involved in the development of your PLN? If so, how? If not would you want their support and how might you want them to support you?	My parents aren't tech savvy so I have to explain some things to them like why having a PLN is important in today's world. They understand and support me 100%
What else do you feel is important in the area of student personal learning networks?	It is important to be known, be heard, and be able to connect with others who understand you. Take your knowledge, go forward, stand out and make sure you can learn how to couple it with what you love.

Educators

In traditional classrooms it is the teacher who is the authority on all knowledge. Empowering students to develop their own knowledge networks can be a bit intimidating and uncomfortable for some educators. **It requires them to continue learning as well, and in so doing to cede some control.** To follow you'll hear from some less-than-traditional teachers and administrators who courageously support their children in developing learning independence via personal learning networks. You'll hear from educators like Ann S. Michaelsen who helps connect her students in Norway to other students around the world using blogs. You'll learn how science teacher Adam Taylor supports students in growing their PLN by following real scientists on Twitter. As you read the insights from these pioneering educators take note of the advice they have for other educators interested in helping their own students develop personal learning networks.

Contributor	
Courtney Woods	Grade 2 Teacher 2012 Microsoft Canada Innovative Teacher Award Winner Bathurst, NB Canada @CourtneyM_Woods
Questions	
Why is it important to support children in the development of personal learning networks?	As an adult, my professional learning network has been absolutely invaluable for my development as an educator. As an early career teacher (5 years in), I want to soak up as much knowledge, expertise, and information as possible. There is no quicker or more effective way to do this than to build my PLN strategically. Whether swapping ideas with a teacher across the hall, engaging in a #2ndchat conversation with my e-colleagues on Twitter, or perusing the blogs of my edu-heroes, the connections I have built with others are always at the forefront of my teaching. Though I may be teaching alone, physically, in a classroom, the influences of those I admire are always present, woven into my lessons and pedagogy and leaving their fingerprints accordingly. Because I value my PLN so, I know that it is especially important for my students to develop their own networks as well - not just within our classroom, or even within our school - but within their communities and online as well. Children need to know that there are many places to go for information, advice, and critiques; there is never just one single holder of knowledge. In a world that is becoming increasingly interconnected via the web, children need to develop the skills necessary to seek out the input of others, and likewise, learn that *their* input is valued and sought out as well.

How do you support children in the development of PLNs?	One way to support children in the development of their PLNs is to showcase examples in how I use mine. I frequently talk about how the lesson we are working on was inspired by another teacher in our school, district, or from around the world. Likewise, when a teacher uses one of our ideas, I share this with my students as a celebration. PLNs are not all about taking ideas; they are about sharing and providing others with knowledge as well. It is a fluid and reciprocal exchange of information. As an early years educator, a large part of my role in helping students develop their PLNs is to provide them with the means to build connections and find information. Seven year olds are naturally full of questions about the world around them, creating the perfect scenarios to begin developing PLNs. A question about tourism led to an award-winning project in which my students used Twitter, Photosynth, and various other platforms to develop a product to be shared with future visitors of our city. Through this project, students chose whom they wanted to contact - celebrities, politicians, the media, and fellow students were popular choices. The excitement when these individuals wrote back was palpable. Their learning became immediately more real and authentic than if it would have been had it simply been shared within the confines of our classroom. A question about Mount Everest led to a student following the blog of a Canadian hiker. Our class asked the hiker questions and he responded, leading to a much richer experience and valuable information than would have been available through a simple Wikipedia search. The children were especially excited when he tweeted us a picture at Mt. Everest Base Camp with a personal shout out to our class.

What advice do you give to students to help them grow their networks?	Follow your passions and get in touch with people who hold knowledge that you want to gain. If you have a question - ask someone who has first hand experience. Watch videos, read books, follow blogs, send an email - there are many different ways that we can access the information we want. The more we learn, the more we want to know. A successful project in my classroom has been our Genius Hour projects (fittingly, an idea I found out about through my PLN, for more information search #geniushour). Based on Google's premise of giving their employees 20% of their time to pursue a personal passion, my students have Friday afternoons to explore whatever they are interested in. These Genius Hour projects have led to deep, real, and engaging learning. Students have sought out their own connections, with my guidance, and developed PLNs based on their own interests. Whether skyping with a paleontologist, emailing a veterinarian, or watching videos on how to maneuver a snowplow, my students are creating PLNs that are rich, motivating, and specifically tailored to them.

Student Personal Learning Networks

What platforms do you recommend and how are each effective?	As a teacher, Twitter has been invaluable in developing my own PLN. I have a core group of second grade teachers with whom I regularly exchange ideas, tips, and information. Twitter has also been a great way for my class to engage with other elementary classrooms. Through our classroom account, we are regularly in contact with other classes. We monitor each other's progress, leave math questions for the others to solve, and cheer on great work. Twitter is a powerful way to receive immediate feedback from a wide variety of sources. My students will tweet the Prime Minister, Bill Gates, the local media, other teachers, and even their parents when they feel especially proud about their work. They will ask questions to authors, mathematicians, biologists, or historians when they are seeking new information. Twitter opens the world up to my students and creates a setting where PLNs can develop naturally. Skype has also been a powerful tool. Through Skype, we have had conversations with several different authors who provide us with tips and techniques to improve our own writing. We have Skyped with a paleontologist, who taught us about fossils and reptiles and local deposits. We have Skyped with other classrooms from around the world during "Mystery Skype" questions, where each class takes turns asking the other questions to try and determine their location in the world. Bottom line, Skype puts students directly in contact with experts who hold a wealth of knowledge and who are eager to pass it on to those who seek it. Other platforms such as Photosynth, Storybirds, KidBlog, and Wiki Spaces have also proved valuable in helping my students develop their PLNs. As an early years educator, a special emphasis is placed on internet safety and creating a digital footprint that is secure and responsible.

How has having a PLN helped your students?	PLNs have helped my students realize that their learning is meaningful. Their questions are valid, and their knowledge is valued. There is a sense of excitement when we learn something new; the students cannot wait to share their progress and information with others. Likewise, when a student has a question, the immediate response is not to look to me for the answer, but to rack our PLNs and determine the best contact to ask and access the information. It is a powerful thing to see seven year olds determine that "Stephen McCranie, the author we Skyped with last week", would be able to help us improve our online cartoons (Bitstrips).
How has your teaching been affected when your students now have their own learning networks?	When my students have their own PLNs, I am no longer the holder of all knowledge (not that I ever was; my students just expected me to be!). I am now holding the role of facilitator, introducing my students to new platforms, how to use them safely, and how to contact those who may help my students learn what they want to know. My job is more exciting. I get to research new ways to create and facilitate these connections for my students. I get to see their eyes spark when they discover the answer to a long burning question. I get to see the sheer thrill when one of their idols contacts them back. I get to promote a classroom where inquiry and the sharing of ideas is not only expected, but valued.

Student Personal Learning Networks

Share a couple of the most powerful examples of how a student's PLN has been of value?	After creating a 360-degree Photosynth of one of our city's landmarks, my students decided to tweet it out to their PLNs. The response was incredible, with former residents, the media, local celebrities, and other teachers re-tweeting it out to their own followers. Our Photosynth now has over 1200 views and as one student excitedly put it, has, in their world, "gone viral!" Our city tourism department currently uses our project to showcase our area to tourists and potential visitors. Tweeting with other classrooms has also been a powerful experience for my students. They swap math problems, showcase writing, provide feedback, record themselves reading, and discover what life is like in another part of the world. I think it is important to teach students that children, not just adults, are valuable members of PLNs and hold important knowledge that can be shared. It is an incredible feeling to know that somewhere, someone else in the world is interested in the same topic as you and is working towards same learning objectives.

Have students met members of their PLN face-to-face? If so, how was that? How did you ensure your students are doing so safely?	When working on their tourism Photosynth project, my students did meet with local celebrities of the web-series "Meredith and Monique, Experience Bathurst". The children had been following their videos and using them as a learning tool for how to promote our area effectively. When Meredith and Monique contacted our classroom and arranged a visit, their PLNs came to life. I contacted Meredith and Monique beforehand to arrange the meeting and it helped that I knew them personally; safety wasn't a huge issue in this case. That being said, internet safety is something that we talk about constantly. We learn that wherever we go, we leave a digital footprint for others to see and therefore must remain professional and responsible. Students use only their initials when posting on Twitter, and their blogs do not contain any personal identifying information. I closely monitor every interaction that each student has online. It is my hope that these lessons remain with my students as they grow older and gain more internet independence.
What is your advice to teachers who want to support their students in developing a PLN?	Begin by tapping into your students' questions, interests, and wonders. How can you help them access information from the experts who hold specific knowledge? Twitter, Skype, blogs and local organizations are a great way to start. I have found that people have been very generous with their time and are more than willing to help my students learn. Whether through an email, a Skype session, or a tweet conversation, there are people all over the world who are eager to share their knowledge with others.
What else do you feel is important to share?	Students need PLNs just as much as adults do. I cannot imagine teaching in a world where I did not have the expertise of many others to draw upon. Likewise, students want, and need, to learn in a world where the exchange of ideas and information happens naturally, fluidly, and authentically.

Student Personal Learning Networks

Contributor	
Angela Maiers @AngelaMaiers	I believe these two words can change the world - #YouMatter I'm an educator, author, and speaker passionate about literacy, learning, and power of social media. Iowa · AngelaMaiers.com
Questions	
Why is it important to support children in the development of personal learning networks?	Learning today is a far more collaborative process than it was even five years ago. While there are many instances of scholarly collaboration throughout history, none rise to the level of what's possible today, where dozens or scores or hundreds of people from around the world can connect simultaneously and in real-time to work on a project. Even when the collaboration is one on one, students have much more access to thought-leaders, experts, and academics in any field than they used to have. As Professor Clay Shirky says, most people "overestimate the value of access to information and underestimate the value of access to each other."
How do you support children in the development of PLNs?	Much the same way I support adults. We know they are first going to follow their friends and favorite celebrities. But then I encourage them to think about their passion, and to connect with people in social media who will fuel that passion. A student who is a history lover and football fan should find, follow and interact with people who are likely to curate and share interesting information about history and football.

What advice do you give to students to help them grow their networks?	Be authentic and transparent. Your online name should be your real name, and no avatars allowed - post an authentic picture of yourself with a description of who you are. Begin to build your own personal brand online - telling people who you really are and what they can expect from you, and then do your best to live up to it. Be kind, be considerate. Reciprocate. Don't talk about yourself all the time. Know that you will make mistakes - we all do - and know they won't be fatal.
What platforms do you recommend and how are each effective?	Yoursphere is a student-friendly place for students to interact with other students from around the world with similar interests. It also has a place for teachers to create a classroom page. Quora can be a great place for students to ask questions and receive answers back from professionals. Twitter and Facebook are the two on which I spend most of my time. Twitter is a platform on which you can have tens of thousands of followers, and use hashtags to interact with them on different topics or at different times. Facebook is more intimate; even if we have several thousand friends, it feels like you're sharing at a deeper level.
How has having a PLN helped your students?	I know so many students who are learning more online than they do in school, and who are creating important professional relationships with adults that will benefit them for years to come, even as they begin their job search.

Student Personal Learning Networks

How has your teaching been affected when your students now have their own learning networks?	While I am no longer in the classroom, I do have the privilege of interacting with students all the time. I know than when I, or any teacher, speaks with students, we are no longer viewed as the sole, or even primary, source of information - students with a learning network can double check anything!
Share a couple of the most powerful examples of how a student's PLN has been of value?	My student friends Ian Coon and Jack Hostager from Waukee, IA created the first student-led learning conference, in Iowa in October. It was an incredible event, organized entirely on social media, and a wonderful learning experience for everyone involved.
Have students met members of their PLN face-to-face? If so, how was that? How did you ensure your students are doing so safely?	The ISLI conference was an extraordinary opportunity for students to meet face-to-face with members of their PLN in a safe setting. Teachers and parents have but to take the same common-sense precautions they've always taken when students interact with adults. The only difference today is that such interactions are much more common.
What is your advice to teachers who want to support their students in developing a PLN?	Encourage them; building a PLN takes time and effort and the payoff is deferred. Build effective communication. Do not feel you need to look over their shoulder or play a "gotcha" game, and do not focus primarily on "what could go wrong." Equip students with information and knowledge and be available to guide them when necessary. This is the same approach we've been taking to letting our students wander out into the world for centuries.

Parents

With our without parents, many young people are growing the personal learning networks. Parents, however, can play an important role in supporting their children in developing and building their networks. Unfortunately, in many cases, they are not doing this and rather leaving the job of learning in the hands of the school or just leaving children to their own devices.

Innovative educators can empower parents to support their children in finding, developing, and growing their passions safely and responsibly via personal learning networks. To follow, you'll hear from some parents who are doing just that. You'll also get advice from parents like Amy Millstein. Her children have robust learning networks with little work from her aside from the encouragement, acknowledgement, and support on which our children thrive. Pay special attention to the advice these parents have for other parents. See what resonates with you and use it to come up with ideas for partnering with parents where you work.

Student Personal Learning Networks

Contributor	
Amy Milstein @greenmangoes	Writer of blog & fiction... not at the same time. Mom of 2 unschooled kids ages 13 and 9 ; yep, you've found the radical fringe. Wife to one very patient guy. New York, NY · unschoolingnyc.com
Questions	
What interest led to the development of your child's PLN?	In my daughter Maya's case, it was a combo of interest in video-making/editing, selling items on line and making video tutorials for crafts. Her network is very fluid - she is no longer in touch with many people, and has changed interests over the years. My son Ben's network is all about Minecraft.
How did it grow?	Organically in both cases, through tutorials and introductions to others via Skype and online communities - in Maya's case a group she found through selling items on YouTube, and in Ben's, a Minecraft chat developed for homeschoolers led to offshoot servers and groups in which he is very active.
What platforms did your child use and how were each of them effective?	YouTube, primarily for Maya, for learning, creating, sharing and even selling items. Minecraft and Skype for Ben.
How did the PLN help your child?	Amazingly, in both cases, their one on one, in person social skills improved by leaps and bounds after they connected with other kids online.

Share a couple of the most powerful examples of how your child's PLN has been of value.	Ben has learned more through Minecraft than I can list here: math, sciences, architecture, circuitry.... Maya has become a great editor and is confident in her ability to find and learn just about anything she wants. In both cases it increased confidence in their own abilities.
Did your child meet members of their PLN face-to-face? If so, how was that? How did you ensure your child was doing so safely?	Maya met a couple of friends during a trip to California - I was with her, as were the parents of the other children. Ben knows some of his Minecraft friends through the homeschooling community and so has met them at homeschool events. Safety was never really an issue. Open lines of communication between parent and child is key in this regard. I've always spoken openly to my kids in an age appropriate way about any and all subjects, so when it came to then internet and online activity, they were aware of the possible (though not necessarily probable) 'dangers' of online interaction and how to avoid or handle them.
Were you involved in the development of your child's PLN? If so, how?	No, not really.
What is your advice to parents who want to support their children in developing a PLN?	Support, but don't push. Suggest, and guide if asked. Try to find ways to say yes instead of immediately showing suspicion and saying no. Then step back and let them roll with it.
What else do you feel is important to share?	Online communities are a fabulous way to meet people with similar interests; my kids have friends all over the world as a result.

Contributor	
Lainie Liberti @ilainie	Nomad, RTW traveler, global citizen, adventurer, conscious spirit, unschooler, blogger, podcaster & mom (+recovered brand specialist) Traveling the World! http://www.raisingmiro.com http://ProjectWorldSchoolPeru.com
Questions	
What interest led to the development of your child's PLN?	Initially my son developed his PLNs through online games like Minecraft and other online gaming communities. From there, he developed friendships that seemed to grow as they grew. However, my son's strongest connections were with kids that were also traveling with their families and unschooling or worldschooling as a form of education. Those similarities created a platform to share experiences and grow some unexpected interests that ultimately are an expansion of learning. For example, my son was talking about the coolest jungles, or city capitals or volcanoes or monuments with his traveling friends and inadvertently learning without effort.
How did it grow?	My son's PLN grew as our community grew through our travel blog RaisingMIro.com We built a strong Facebook community and have a ton of engagement through Facebook, our blog and Skype. Being a traveling unschooler is isolating and as my son now enters his teen years, he's feeling this isolation more deeply. Together, both my son and I are seeking to grow our PLNs through creating temporary learning communities throughout the world, first being where we currently are: Peru.

What platforms did your child use and how were each of them effective?	The digital platforms my son uses is primarily Skype to connect one to one and for learning, my son loves multiple learning communities surround Youtubers (Vsauce + gamers). I use our blog, Twitter and Facebook more to share information and pass it along to my son.
How did the PLN help your child?	The PLNs help my son to retain a feeling of connectedness. That is his primary concern. Learning happens passively as he seeks information independently as he researches & discovers new things effortlessly. Then connecting with others through his personal network on Skype helps him share, process and build upon the new information. PLNs are a necessary part of learning as we've discovered learning is social.
Share a couple of the most powerful examples of how your child's PLN has been of value.	When my son was younger, he connected with many people via Minecraft. That was one of his most influential learning tools. It exposed him to multiplayer collaboration. What he learned through those experiences was extensive. He learned how to engage in multiplayer online communities and share and develop friendships. Now my son is interested in writing. He's engaged in online and offline writing groups. He's working now on a book through a collaborative group, also contributing to this project. They use Skype to connect weekly and have an ongoing Google document that they edit, write and share ideas. I think the process presents more value than the actual project, since I see development in negotiation, give and take and compromise as one of the huge benefits.

Did your child meet members of their PLN face-to-face? If so, how was that? How did you ensure your child was doing so safely?	In terms of the writing group, my son has only met one of the persons in his group face-to-face. That connection was initially made at an unschooling conference. The rest of my son's connections are virtual and have not met face to face. I don't think there are safety issues since all connections are from either the unschooling community or the travel community.
Were you involved in the development of your child's PLN? If so, how?	Yes. Completely. We built a PLN quite by accident. We started our journey as travelers and after 8 months of travel, we decided to blog about our journey. Through sharing our lives, the ups and downs of travel, sharing about our relationship and eventually writing about learning in the context of travel we started to develop a loyal and engaged audience. Through that audience, my son then developed PLNs through connecting with other traveling-unschooling kids his age.
What is your advice to parents who want to support their children in developing a PLN?	I would say trust and support your kids and encourage them to develop online friendships with other kids similar to themselves. We've found that creating community is one's strongest support mechanisms to learning. Through those bonds, learning happens. I've witnessed it time and time again.
What else do you feel is important to share?	Don't be afraid to embrace technology as the seed to creating PLNs. But, I have to urge, face-to-face community engagement should be one of the goals. Learning through community (online or not) is one of the strongest contributors to immersive learning. The peer feedback loop is crucial and through online connections, one gets to practice interpersonal communication.

Contributor	
Kelly Raudenbush @myoverthinking	Mother of two boys and two girls, cofounder of the nonprofit The Sparrow Fund supporting adoptive families, and Philadelphia area blogger at www.myoverthinking.com
Questions	
What interest led to the development of your child's PLN?	I'm a mother of four - two of whom have special needs - one of those has an individualized education plan (IEP) and one has a gifted individualized education plan (GIEP). I learned quickly that there were lots of resources for my child with an IEP. But, my child with a GIEP seemed to be held back educationally–the resources and attention she needed to challenge her and advance her just weren't there. She needed more.
How did it grow?	Because she wanted it to! At 9 years old, she took initiative to start using the Internet to advance on her own.
What platforms did your child use and how were each of them effective?	My 9 year old has been very actively using Google docs to "meet up" with friends to work on projects together. Probably most heartwarming to me is finding my son with special needs on one computer working on a chapter book he was writing on his own with my daughter, 2 years younger than him, on the other computer logged into Google docs editing his writing as he goes. My two children on different sides of the educational bell curves working together = brilliant. My 9 year old also started her own online business this year on Etsy (www.beaditfordisney.etsy.com). She took a creative idea she had, learned how to take and edit pictures with mom's help, learned how to post new listings online and how to promote them.

	While learning how to track her income and profits in Excel, she's also been learning digital citizenship as she answers questions, talks to customers, and emails people about custom orders. This real life classroom has served her better than any established curriculum she's had lately.
How did the PLN help your child?	She takes great pride in her ability to create PowerPoint presentations to show her family and friends how to "do something" or teach the rest of us who don't know the ins and outs of the rides at Disney World, for example. And, she takes great pride in her mastery of Google docs. And, her confidence has grown tremendously as an entrepreneur and business owner.
Did your child meet members of their PLN face-to-face? If so, how was that? How did you ensure your child was doing so safely?	She has never met anyone she has engaged with online in person–yet. But, I have coached her about what she should share and not share, and how to conduct herself online. With a mother who blogs, she is well aware of what a digital footprint is.
Were you involved in the development of your child's PLN? If so, how?	Absolutely. Thought I confess that she's taught me as much about engaging online as I have taught her!
What is your advice to parents who want to support their children in developing a PLN?	Allow your child to see the open door that developing a PLN can give to him or her and then encourage him or her to take the initiative and develop what it can look like for them. Be present for it but don't let your presence and involvement get in the way of his or her own creativity.
What else would you like to share?	As a parent, be a learner as well as a guide!

Contributor	
Lisa Nalbone @lisanalbone	Lisa shares her experience from teaching, community organizing, unschooling, and raising Dale Stephens, founder of UnCollege by offering tips, resources and consulting at LisaNalbone.com
Questions	
What interest led to the development of your child's PLN?	Writing, art, music, business, community organizing, politics, social interaction
How did it grow?	My son's learning network initially grew through our local community, personal friendships, volunteering, community groups like 4H, local homeschool groups and activities. As a teen (maybe 16) Dale made connections at conferences. He kept them up, and expanded them with Twitter, Facebook and email. As Dale wanted/needed more targeted resources we still began with local references. We grew and extended connections via social media like Twitter and Facebook. We also reached out to professionals to find internships, advice for biz and publishing.
What platforms did your child use and how were each of them effective?	He started with face to face then advanced to using social media long before I was. Various face-to-face and online platforms have been effective and can be used in different ways. For example, Dale has used Twitter to reach out to authors, media people and other "higher status" folks to initiate a conversation which can then be followed up with email or other further contact. However it was a local contact that made his literary agent connection. That first connection came from a notice at the post office.

How did the PLN help your child?	The PLN introduced Dale to opportunities and mentoring beyond the skill/experience of his parents. It helped to broaden his experiences, access to resources and offered ways to see how other people approached life. Just for context, we were not very tech/internet savvy and did not have a computer or internet service until Dale was about 7. It was an extremely limited dial-up service. Online was not our first source of information like it is now. During Dale's unschooling years (10 - 17 years old) we helped with several family members' terminal battles with cancer. Having a strong PLN and community was especially helpful to Dale and us during these times.
Share a couple of the most powerful examples of how your child's PLN has been of value.	Face-to-face connections have proven valuable. When Dale was about 15 he wanted more expert input on his writing than I could provide and he worked with a mom from our homeschool group. This really improved Dale's writing skills and love of writing which led to writing Hacking Your Education. A PLN member of his French conversation group led to a good literary agent and a great source of support. Twitter and Facebook were very important when Dale first started the UnCollege website and he was trying to promote and get feedback on his ideas. He would Tweet a link to his articles and ask specific people for feedback. This helped him get a lot of the beginning publicity for his ideas.

Did your child meet members of their PLN face-to-face. If so, how was that? How did you ensure your child was doing so safely?	Yes. Face-to-face meetings were good. First meetings would be in public spaces, and preferably in a group. I also would meet other parents or adults involved - for example a potential ride-share person, when the French group moved from public library meetings to home based meetings. We discussed safety issues, such as not going off with individuals, keeping in contact about his plans and locations, trying to get references and background information about people or organizations and we made plans for checking-in and often a contingency for who else I could contact or, god forbid, when to send in the troops. (I also have to do this with my hubby when he hikes alone.)
Were you involved in the development of your child's PLN? If so, how?	Yes. I was involved in the development of my child's PLN early on. I helped with looking for mentors, other guidance, and connections. As a teen I received great value from what would now be called a PLN that helped me learn/experience beyond the resources and education my parents had to offer. I knew how valuable it was to have adult connections beyond school teachers. I wanted that kind of extra support for my child. I believe that learning, child-rearing and community are intertwined, so I actively tried to create a wider community even before Dale was born. Truly I would say Dale's PLN began with our friend Rosemary, who was a doctoral student when Dale was born and took care of him once a week, often on campus, for a few of his early years. She is now a sociology professor and is still an active member of his PLN. Our PLN development continued with strong connection to Dale's preschool teacher Jan who morphed into close friend and an art and business mentor for Dale.

	Dale would express interest and we would brainstorm about the people we knew or could contact who might help in that area. We had a fantastic homeschool group and the other parents were all very generous about being part of Dale's PLN. Members of our small town community were also very willing to participate. At first I was scared about Dale reaching out on social media sites like Twitter but quickly saw the incredible value, especially since we were somewhat isolated in a small rural community. He developed his online PLN on his own.
What is your advice to parents who want to support their children in developing a PLN?	It is worth the effort. Make time in your life to develop PLN for yourself and to support your child in developing a PLN. They may need or want modeling and guidance to begin with. Parents need to be unafraid of letting your children grow beyond you. There are so many incredible opportunities and ways to connect. We really started pre-internet and social media, which is still a valuable way to start. But with the internet communities the world is at your doorstep. Side-by-side internet use, Twitter chats, attending and participating in virtual conferences can all lead to great PLN connections.
What else do you feel is important to share?	Every person and interaction is a potential source of learning - even though we may not imagine ahead of time what we will learn. Everyone has something to share whether or not they have credentials or are considered an "expert." Perhaps a neighbor has a great recipe, insights from when they were in the Japanese internment camps, or may be able to introduce you to just the right person you need for a PLN down the road. Don't discount anyone as a potential source of learning and connection. The earlier you model this attitude with your children or students, the sooner they can appreciate the value of and start developing their own PLN.

Contributor	
Dana Britt | @Dana_Britt	**Parent, Writer & Educator** Dana Britt --website We live a school-free life, learning by living.

Questions	
What interest led to the development of your child's PLN?	Living life leads to connections. Connections were being made naturally, all her life, whatever her interests–from Disney to animé, to childcare and culinary pursuits. We've built her PLN by naturally exploring her every interest, not one particular one. With each new interest, she built on what was already there as well as reaching for new information and connections.
How did it grow?	It has grown, and continues to grow as she lives and explores. I think it is a lifetime pursuit for us all. I talk to everyone, and as she has grown, so does she. She is not afraid to ask questions, shadow people when permitted and research her interests to find new ways to connect/interact. For example, at the used book store, the owner talked about trying to find time to set up a searchable database and my daughter offered to spend a few hours helping on a volunteer basis, knowing the store couldn't afford to hire help. Through that project, she met several people and made new connections. Or we might be out to supper at a restaurant, and she'll ask questions of the server about their job there–which might lead to a 'field trip' or even shadowing, depending on the situation. My part in this was simply being the type to talk to people, to ask questions, to include the kids– showing them how connections can be made. By being willing to talk to people in everyday environments, she builds relationships and thus PLN connections.

What platforms did your child use and how were each of them effective?	The platforms she has used in addition to face-to-face have been online forums regarding specific interests and Facebook groups . They have been effective, in that she has learned how to purposively connect and then later see how a connection is beneficial to her. Some connections have led to childcare jobs while others have led to 'shadowing' people in their respective roles and still others simply sources of information or social connection.
How did the PLN help your child? .	The biggest benefit, and it is the big one–is the building of lifetime connections followed by the gleaning of information: the building of knowledge base .By talking to others, asking questions and seeing their experiences, she is learning an about life, about specific things. But I think the general learning –the building a base of knowledge is the key. What ever she decides to do in life, her connections and base will be there for her to draw from–and she is willing and able to seek out new information and connections.
Share a couple of the most powerful examples of how your child's PLN has been of value.	Her PLN has been of value chiefly for the base of knowledge she is building through connections. Building a life experience, if you will. That being said, my daughter has also shadowed others in their careers to learn about fields such as cake design, wedding planning, child-care and culinary skills. She has learned how there are many variables that affect the outcome of the work being done. Variables in the form of clients, weather, materials and so forth. This is valuable because it allows her to see for herself rather than being merely instructed to be alert for variables. She has found folks to shadow through daily life, neighbors, co-workers of Dad's, parents of children she's cared for, friends with common interests in online groups. She stays connected with such people via email, Facebook and face-to-face visits.

Did your child meet members of their PLN face-to-face. If so, how was that? How did you ensure your child was doing so safely?	As I mentioned, a big part of her PLN is simply the people she meets on a daily basis. In addition, she has met face-to-face, shadowed a neighbor at her job designing, setting up and serving wedding cakes, and arranged a meet up with a friend from a FB group to talk about common interests. For safety, her father and I were present both times for the initial meeting. Once everyone was comfortable, she was in charge of what she wanted to do from there.
Were you involved in the development of your child's PLN? If so, how?	I think the biggest way we have been involved is by daily life, by talking to others, researching information when we wanted to know something, all with her right there, living life with us. Then, as she began to express her interests, we were– and continue to be –supportive of her pursuits. If we see an opportunity or resource, we might mention it to her, but the connection is hers to make if she wants to. If she wants our help, we give it.
What is your advice to parents who want to support their children in developing a PLN?	These connections can be made in a natural fashion, so you don't need to force them– open communication and doors but don't hammer the pavement so to speak. Be supportive and be involved as much as needed in regards to your child's age/ability. If the child is older, try to step back and allow her to build the connections herself, only chiming in when asked or clearly needed.
What else do you feel is important to share?	Building a network is natural when you are living life if you are open to folks, to experiences.

As we've seen from the students, parents, and educators featured here, supporting young people in developing their PLNs greatly benefits their projects and pursuits. Take the practical advice shared by those in this chapter. You can start by helping young people discover their interests. Once they do, guide them in finding those who share their interests in your community as well as in online spaces like Twitter, blogs, and Facebook. Model these techniques by pursuing your own interests and PLN. Guide them in responsible interaction and make sure you let them know at all times you are there to keep them safe.

With these strategies in mind, the young people in your life will be well on their way to taking ownership of their learning by connecting with a community at once local and global designed to explore whatever it is that may be of interest.

www.ingramcontent.com/pod-product-compliance
Lightning Source LLC
Chambersburg PA
CBHW052125070526
44586CB00016B/2088